Garfield
Who's Talking?

JIM DAVIS

℞℞
Ravette Limited

Copyright © 1984
United Feature Syndicate, Inc.
GARFIELD Comic Strips © 1982, 1983, 1984

This edition first published by
Ravette Limited 1984
Reprinted 1985

Printed and bound in Great Britain
for Ravette Limited,
12 Star Road, Partridge Green,
Horsham, Sussex RH13 8RA
by Cox & Wyman Ltd, Reading

ISBN 0 906710 61 8

© 1984 United Feature Syndicate, Inc.

JIM DAVIS

HEY, GARFIELD, DON'T EAT THE LASAGNA YET...

1-7-84   © 1983 United Feature Syndicate, Inc

IT'S STILL TOO HOT

YOU'RE TELLING ME?!

© 1984 United Feature Syndicate, Inc.

WHAT WOULD YOU LIKE FOR CHRISTMAS, AUNT GUSSIE?

OH... NOTHING MUCH

JIM DAVIS

11-11

MAYBE SOMETHING FOR MY BED LIKE A LITTLE LACEY THROW PILLOW

STUFFED WITH JOHN TRAVOLTA'S CHEST HAIR

© 1983 United Feature Syndicate, Inc.

HERE'S ONE OF THE GREAT MYSTERIES OF THE UNIVERSE...

WHEN ODIE CLOSES HIS MOUTH, WHERE DOES HIS TONGUE GO?

5-21

© 1984 United Feature Syndicate, Inc.

HEY, GARFIELD. WE'RE GOING TO THE FARM TO VISIT DAD AND MOM THIS WEEK

3-12   JIM DAVIS

GOODO. I NEED A CHANGE OF SURROUNDINGS. I WAS GETTING BORED WITH THIS CITY LIFE

© 1984 United Feature Syndicate, Inc.

IT WILL BE NICE TO BE BORED IN THE COUNTRY FOR A CHANGE

3-14

© 1984 United Feature Syndicate, Inc.

GARFIELD AND I MUST BE LEAVING NOW, MOM

STAY, STAY! I JUST BAKED SOME PIES

3-17   JIM DAVIS

WE GOTTA GO. COME ON, GARFIELD

© 1984 United Feature Syndicate, Inc.

SAY WHAT, STRANGER?

© 1984 United Feature Syndicate, Inc.

© 1984 United Feature Syndicate, Inc.

© 1984 United Feature Syndicate, Inc.

5-19 JIM DAVIS

© 1984 United Feature Syndicate,Inc

WHIRRR

GARFIELD

J°M DAV°S   11-17

GLUP

PLOP

GARFIELD

© 1983 United Feature Syndicate, Inc.

HOW'S YOUR CAT FOOD, GARFIELD?

I COULD SAY MORE FOR THE PRESENTATION

GARFIELD

THIS IS CALLED A BIRD FEEDER, GARFIELD

JIM DAVIS 2-25

AND THIS IS CALLED PUTTING BIRDSEED INTO THE BIRD FEEDER

HE CAN CALL IT WHAT HE LIKES. I CALL IT BAITING THE TRAP

© 1983 United Feature Syndicate, Inc.

HERE WE ARE IN A REAL FACTORY, BOYS AND GIRLS. LET'S SEE WHAT WE CAN LEARN...

ARRRRRGH!

WHAP! WHAP! WHAP!

© 1984 United Feature Syndicate, Inc.

JiM DAViS 6-6

SHUT THIS ∂☆⚡※ THING OFF

UNCLE ROY IS LEARNING NEVER TO WEAR LOOSE CLOTHING AROUND BIG MACHINERY

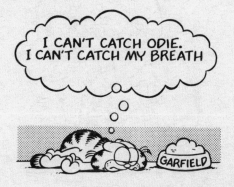

© 1983 United Feature Syndicate, Inc.

© 1983 United Feature Syndicate, Inc.

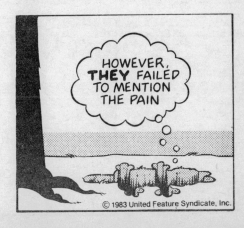

© 1983 United Feature Syndicate, Inc.

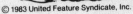

© 1982 United Feature Syndicate, Inc.

HOW MUCH ARE THE PLANE TICKETS?... UH, DO YOU HAVE ANYTHING CHEAPER?

JIM DAVIS

THAT COULD BE FATAL!

4-19

I DON'T THINK THEY WANT OUR BUSINESS, GARFIELD

WHERE'S THE COMPETITION FOR THE LOW ROLLERS THESE DAYS?

© 1984 United Feature Syndicate, Inc.

4-20

HEY! WE'RE GETTING HUNGRY BACK HERE IN THIRD-CLASS! WHAT'S TO EAT?!

JIM DAVIS 4-24

BLAT!

BLAT!

HARDTACK AND SWILL. YUM-YUM

CONK!

CONK!

I KNOW THIS IS JUST THE THIRD-CLASS EXIT FROM THE PLANE, GARFIELD...

JIM DAVIS 4-26

BUT YOU'D THINK THEY'D GIVE US A LADDER OR SOMETHING

© 1984 United Feature Syndicate, Inc.

OH, NO! I HIT AN OLD LADY IN THE HEAD AND KNOCKED HER OUT COLD!

WHAT SHOULD I DO, GARFIELD?!

I'D STRAIGHTEN THAT LEFT ARM A BIT AND TURN THAT RIGHT HAND OVER MORE

JIM DAVIS

1-4-84

OH, NO! IT'S THE OLD "DISGUISE THE TONGUE AS A LOAF OF FRENCH BREAD" TRICK!

© 1983 United Feature Syndicate, Inc.

© 1983 United Feature Syndicate, Inc.

© 1983 United Feature Syndicate, Inc.

© 1984 United Feature Syndicate, Inc.

12-14 © 1983 United Feature Syndicate, Inc.

© 1984 United Feature Syndicate, Inc.

© 1984 United Feature Syndicate, Inc.

© 1984 United Feature Syndicate, Inc.

© 1984 United Feature Syndicate, Inc.

4-7

© 1983 United Feature Syndicate, Inc.

JIM DAVIS   5-18

CHUG!

YOU'RE A REAL BEAR UNTIL YOU'VE HAD YOUR FIRST CUP OF COFFEE, AREN'T YOU?

AND THEN I'M THE SWEETEST SO-AND-SO AROUND

© 1982 United Feature Syndicate, Inc.

OTHER GARFIELD BOOKS IN THIS SERIES

All these books are available at your local bookshop or newsagent, or can be ordered direct from the publisher. Just tick the titles you require and fill in the form below.

Prices and availability subject to change without notice.

Ravette Limited, 12 Star Road, Partridge Green, Horsham, West Sussex RH13 8RA

Please send cheque or postal order, and allow the following for postage and packing. U.K. 45p for one book, plus 20p for the second and 14p for each additional book ordered up to a £1.63 maximum.

Name ....

Address ....

....